Big Machines
in Emergencies

Geoff Thompson

Contents

Emergency vehicles

Emergency vehicles help keep people safe.

They are used when people are sick
or hurt or in danger.

All emergency vehicles can go very fast.

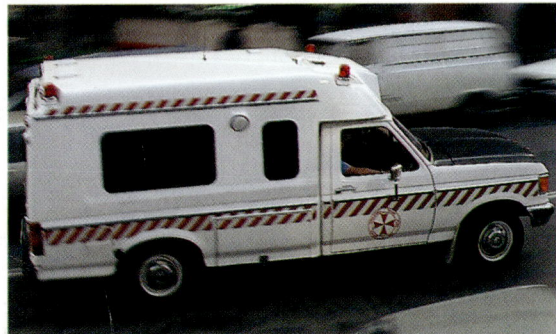

It is easy to know
when emergency vehicles are coming.
They have sirens and flashing lights.
They have bright markings, too.

Other drivers have to make way
for emergency vehicles.

Fire trucks

Fire trucks are bright red.
They have very loud sirens.

When people hear the siren,
they stop and make way for the fire truck.

DID YOU KNOW?

In a city,
firefighters can get water
from a hydrant
at the side of the road.

Fire rescue

Fire trucks have long ladders
that reach up the sides of tall buildings.

Firefighters climb up the ladders
to rescue people
and spray water on the fire.

If there is a fire at home ...

1. Shout "FIRE!"
to tell everyone.

2. Get down low
and go, go, go!

3. Get outside quickly.

4. Don't go back
into the burning house.

Fire boats

Fire boats put out fires on ships,
and in buildings that are near the water.

Fire boats pump water
from the river or the sea.
They spray water on the fire.

Fire helicopters

Helicopters are used to put out fires in the forest or the bush.

A big bucket hangs under the helicopter and drops water on the fire.

Ambulances

Ambulances are white with red markings. They have flashing lights and sirens, too.

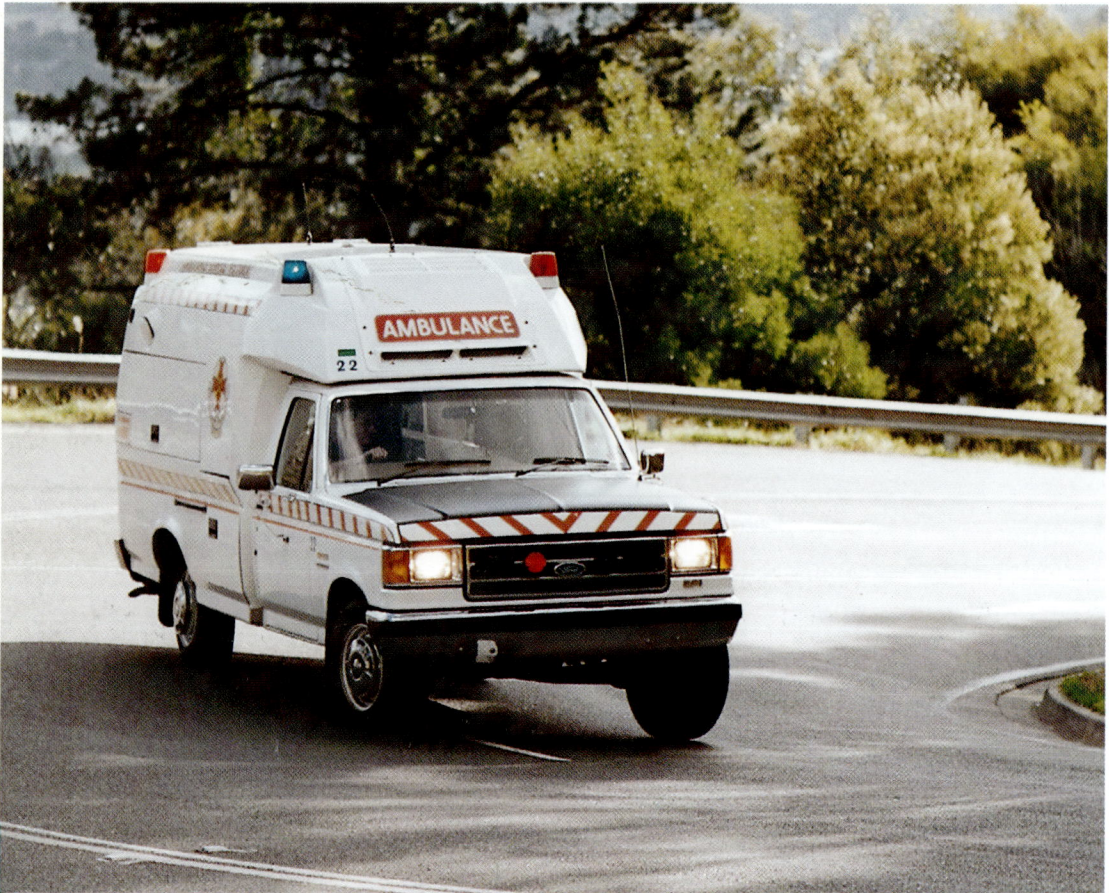

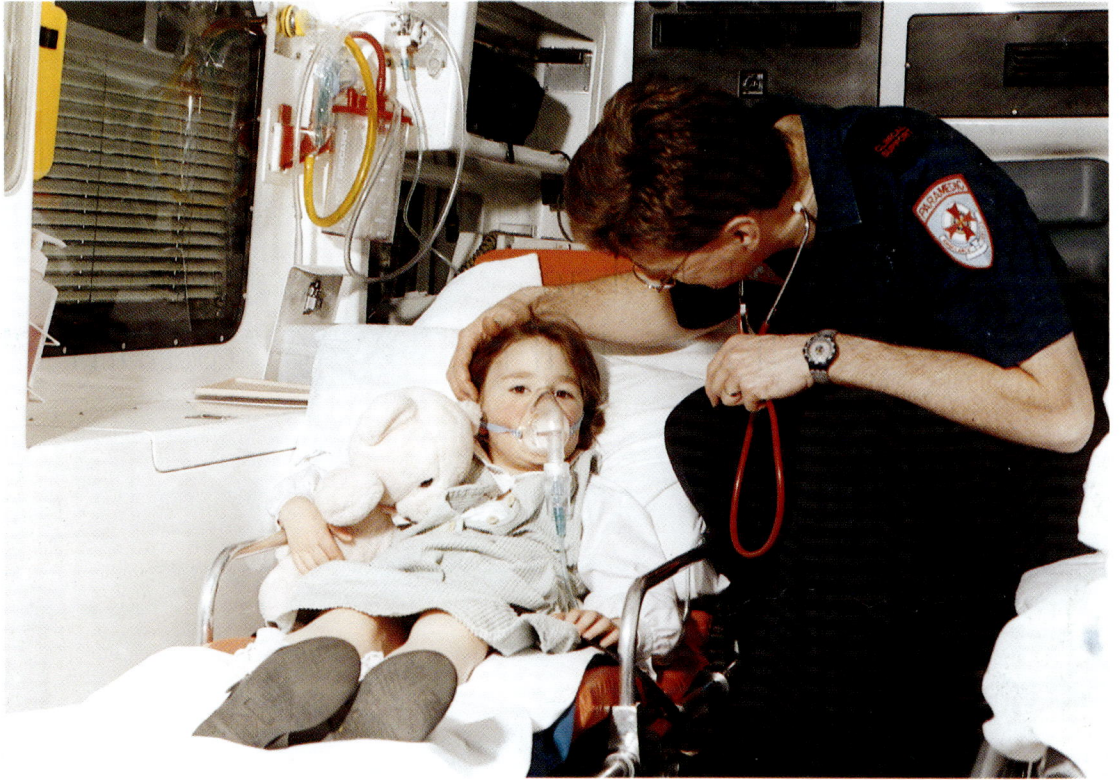

An ambulance takes sick or hurt people to the hospital.

Air ambulances

Planes can be used
to fly sick or hurt people very quickly
from one place to another.
They are called air ambulances.

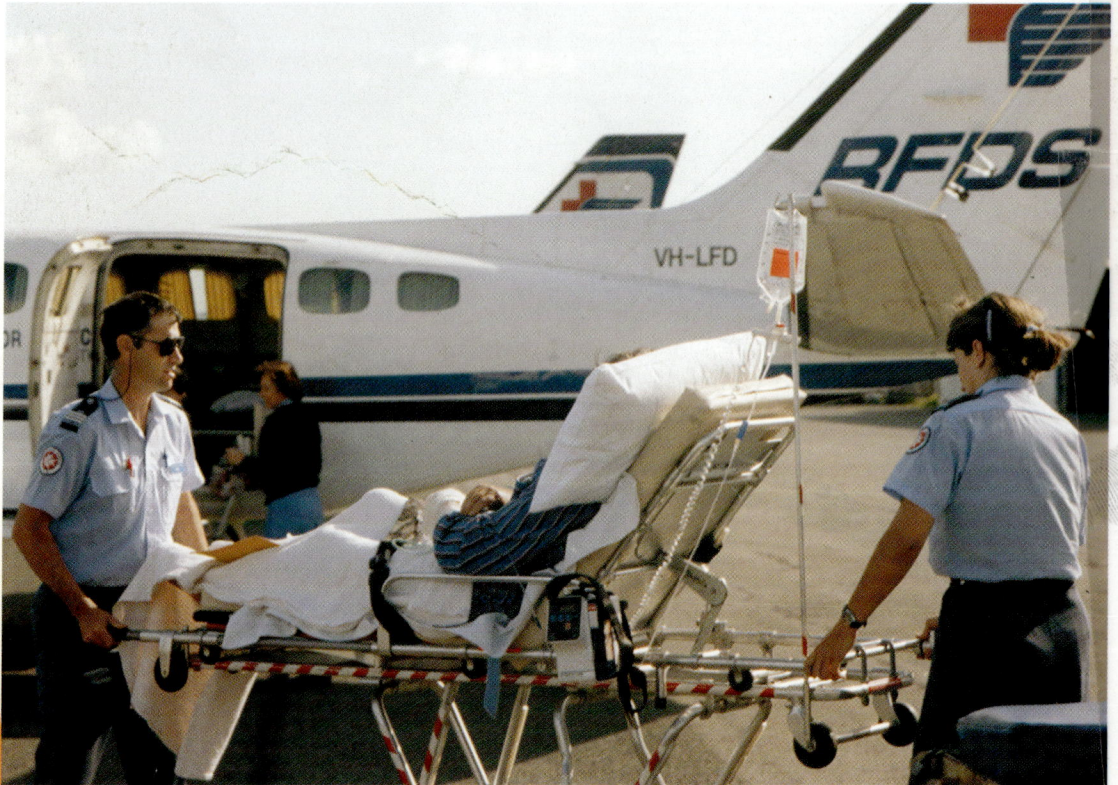

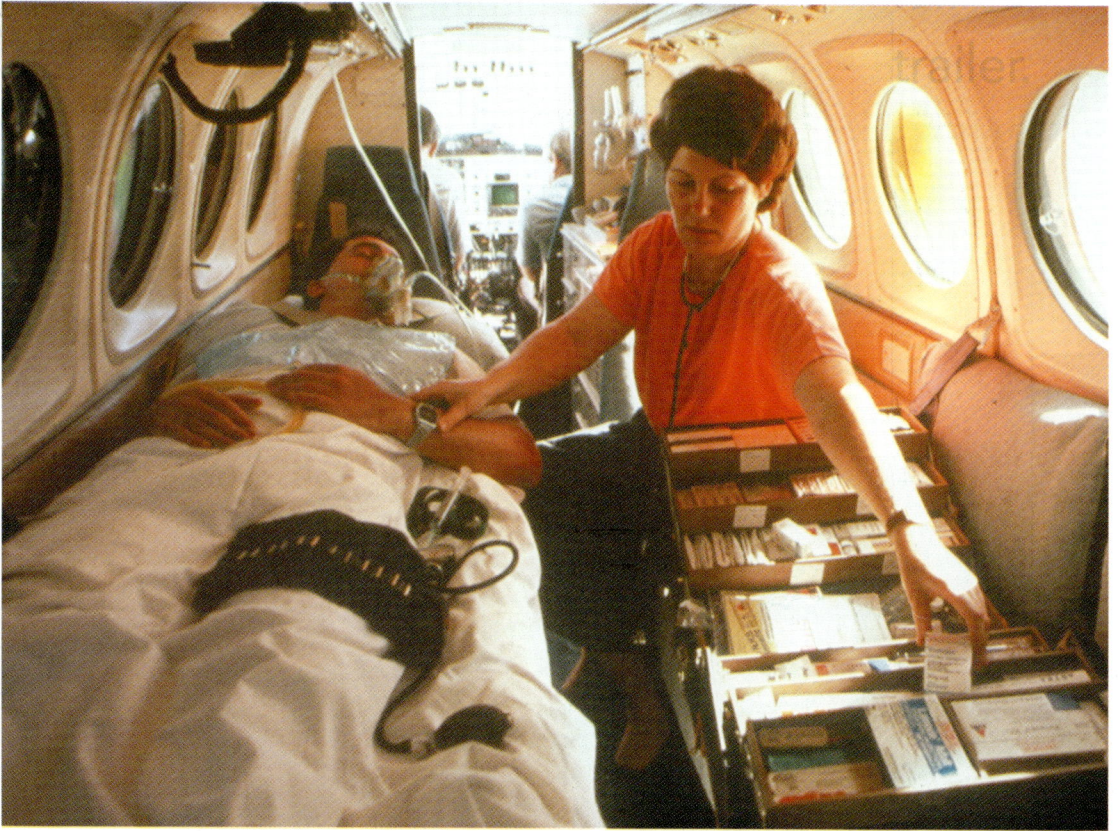

The sick people lie on a bed
in the back of the plane.

Snow ambulances

A snow ambulance can go over ice and snow.

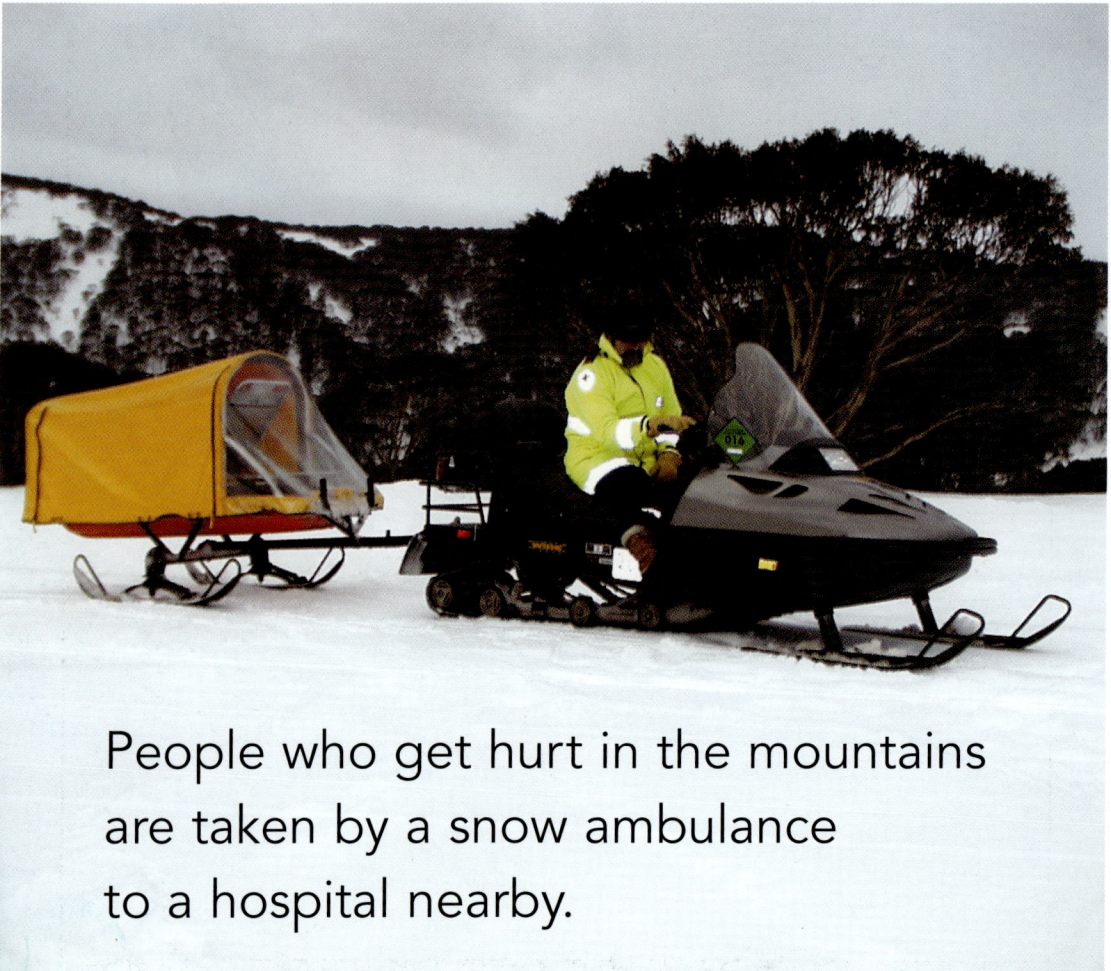

People who get hurt in the mountains
are taken by a snow ambulance
to a hospital nearby.

Dear Meg,
Last week, when I was playing
in the snow,
I fell over and broke my leg.
The snow ambulance
had to come and get me!
They put me on a special bed
in the sled of the ambulance.

Your friend,
Katie

Police cars

Police cars are white with blue markings.

When they are going to an emergency,
police cars go very fast.
Their sirens and red and blue flashing lights
are turned on.

Police cars go to help
fire trucks, ambulances
and other emergency vehicles.

DID YOU KNOW?

Police have two-way radios
to talk to other police cars
and to home base.

Police helicopters

Sometimes police use helicopters
as well as cars.

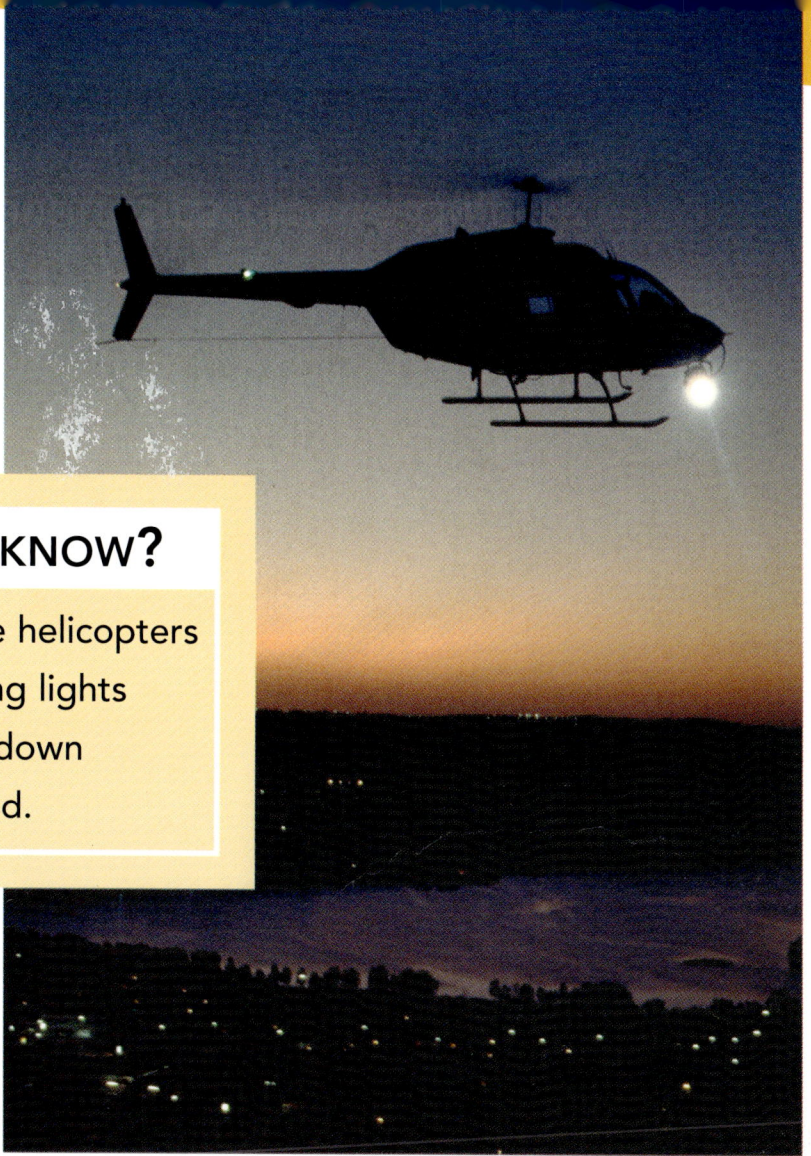

DID YOU KNOW?

At night, police helicopters
have very strong lights
that can shine down
onto the ground.

From up in the helicopter,
they can see many things
that police in cars cannot see.

Police boats

Police boats have big motors
and can go very fast.
Police boats are used
to stop other boats and people
from getting into danger on the water.

Sometimes police boats are used
to look for people
who are lost at sea or in rivers.

Questions

1. Where do firefighters get water from, in a city?

2. What can police use when they want to talk to other police cars or to home base?

3. What do police helicopters use at night?

Glossary

danger	*something that could hurt you*
fire hydrant	*a pipe on the side of the road where firefighters get water*
siren	*a loud sound to warn people*
vehicle	*a machine that carries people or goods*